PRAYERBOOK FOR ENGAGED COUPLES

PRAYERBOOK FOR ENGAGED COUPLES

Second Edition, with Readings
from the Revised Lectionary

Austin Fleming

LITURGY
TRAINING
PUBLICATIONS

Austin Fleming is a priest of the archdiocese of Boston. He is pastor of Our Lady, Help of Christians parish, in Concord, Massachusetts.

PRAYERBOOK FOR ENGAGED COUPLES, SECOND EDITION © 2004, 1990, Archdiocese of Chicago: Liturgy Training Publications, 1800 North Hermitage Avenue, Chicago IL 60622; 1-800-933-1800, fax 1-800-933-7094, e-mail orders@ltp.org. All rights reserved. See our Web site at www.LTP.org.

This book was edited by Victoria M. Tufano. Carol Mycio was the production editor. The cover design is by Larry Cope; the interior is based on a design created by Ana Aguilar-Islas. The typesetting was done by Jim Mellody-Pizzato in Goudy.

Printed in the United States of America.

Library of Congress Control Number: 2003115602

ISBN-10: 1-56854-520-7
ISBN-13: 978-1-56854-520-2

PWED2

For Gerry and Kristin

CONTENTS

FOREWORD

M OST people pray. Usually alone. Usually in their own words. And that is good. But you are getting married. Your lives will be lived together. Perhaps children will share the life of the household you two will make. So this book suggests that you can pray together as well as individually. It suggests that in addition to your own words of prayer, you pray and reflect on words that belong to you because you are the church. These words come directly from the wedding liturgy. One by one and all together, they are about the better and the worse, the richer and the poorer, the "death do us part." They might help you talk about things that easily get swept aside in the details of planning your wedding. They might build a foundation for prayer and serious conversation together after marriage.

HOW TO USE THIS BOOK

THIS is a prayer book for engaged couples. It is a guide for preparing to celebrate your marriage as a Christian sacrament. This prayer book is based on several assumptions:

- that you believe in God who is love
- that you believe God is the source of your love for your partner
- that you believe God hears and answers your prayer

It is also assumed that you *want* to pray. Most of us fall into this category of people who *want* to pray—but many of us don't know how or where to begin. This book won't do the praying for you, but it will help you get started. These pages are designed to help bring to your lips what is in your mind and heart as you stand before the Lord who will join you together as one in the sacrament of marriage.

This prayer book is written for you and your partner to use together. You will need some quiet time in a quiet place, together. This kind of time doesn't fall into our laps out of nowhere—you will need to *make* the time for prayer together. Prayer is intimate, personal. But that does not mean it must be private. *Sharing* prayer with another person, before God, is a moment of intimacy. To stand together before God, to open your hearts to the one who knows the secrets of your hearts, to bare your needs and fears and joys and hopes—this is a sharing of intimacies that sometimes runs deeper than the sharing of yourselves in making love. Your shared prayer as an engaged and married couple is a unique opportunity for sharing your love for each other and for coming to know your God.

Most of us are not accustomed to praying out loud with one other person, so don't be surprised or discouraged if things are awkward at first. There are no right or wrong words. Simply taking the time to pray together is better than eloquence. As husband and wife you will be sharing yourselves in intimate ways; if your faith and your prayer can be shared, all else will take on new meaning.

Like any prayer book, this one is meant to give you a nudge in the right direction and a few words to begin. The first words of each unit of prayer are taken from the marriage ritual as it is celebrated in the Roman Catholic Church. These are some of the texts that will be proclaimed and prayed at your wedding. As you pray with this book you will become more familiar with the words and gestures that will form your wedding liturgy. More than any commentary, these words themselves beautifully announce what the church has to say about Christian marriage. The words come in many forms—stories, poems, prayers, commands, invitations, blessings—but all of them are worth pondering both before and after the celebration of your wedding.

STEP BY STEP

The main part of this book consists of 32 "prayer starters." Each one follows this format:

1. a scripture passage or ritual element from the marriage liturgy
2. a brief reflection on that text
3. several comments or questions to help you ponder the text

4. several intercessions for the needs of others and for your own needs
5. a concluding prayer
6. the Lord's Prayer

In all, 32 texts have been chosen from the wedding ritual of the church; 20 of these are scripture (introduced on page 7) and 12 of them are other texts from the rite (page 49).

Using the creation account in Genesis as an example (page 8), Mary and John might pray together in this way:

- Together, John and Mary make the sign of the cross.
- Mary reads aloud the scripture passage. *Be sure to read the text with attention and expression.*
- Mary and John spend some quiet time to reflect on the passage. *Allow at least a couple of minutes of silence for reflection. Sometimes reading the passage again after this silence brings it new life.*
- John reads aloud the reflection, then the questions.
- Mary and John respond to the reflection and questions. *Take as much time as you need and want for this conversation. Again, repeating the reading will reveal things not heard before.*
- Mary reads the intercessions.
- John and Mary add "the needs we name this day . . ." *Add the needs of the world, of your families and friends, and your own needs.*
- John reads the prayer that begins: "God, creator of heaven and earth." *Pray the words slowly; don't rush.*
- John and Mary pray together the Lord's Prayer (or one of the other prayers found in the section "Other Prayers and Blessings" at the back of this book).

Be sure to alternate in reading the several parts each time you pray—especially if one of you tends to be less vocal in your prayer together. Formal prayers help us to pray when we cannot find our own words or when our own words are difficult to speak.

If distance separates you, make plans to pray over the same passage, perhaps at a particular time of the day, and to share your thoughts in letters or e-mails, through keeping a journal, talking over the telephone, or when you are together.

At the back of the book are additional prayer texts for use when you pray alone or together. You will also find two simple prayer services (one for blessing an engaged couple, one for blessing a son or daughter just before the wedding celebration). These are for you and your families to use.

What better way to prepare for marriage than to learn to pray together, using the words of scripture and of the church's ritual, praising God for all you have been given and asking God's blessings upon all that is to come.

Your prayer together may flow more easily on some days than others. Some passages may lead you to prayer more easily than others. Do not give up on the days when prayer is difficult—these may be the days when you most need to speak to the Lord. And do not skip over the more difficult selections—these may be the words you most need to ponder together. Feel free to ask any-one who is helping in your marriage preparation for assistance in learning to pray together.

This book can be used over and over again. You might pray through all the texts three or four times before your wedding day. The words of scripture and prayer never cease to reveal more and more of our relationship with one another and with God. Even after you have celebrated your wedding and are no longer "engaged" but now husband and wife, these texts can still serve your prayer together. Use this book to celebrate the good times and to seek God's help and strength in the bad times—all the days of your life.

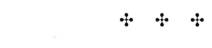

SCRIPTURE READINGS

T his section offers a number of the scripture passages that may be proclaimed at wedding celebrations in the Roman Catholic Church. These are taken from the Hebrew Scriptures (the Old Testament), from the gospels, and from the letters found in the Christian Scriptures (the New Testament).

These passages speak of love: of God's creative and saving love, of the love we are to have for one another, and of the ways in which married love is to be an image of God's love for humankind and the whole of creation.

Let the word of God, rich as it is, dwell and take root in you!

Very, very good!

THEN God said:
"Let us make man in our image, after our likeness.
Let them have dominion over the fish of the sea,
    the birds of the air, and the cattle,
    and over all the wild animals
    and all the creatures that crawl on the ground."

God created man in his image;
    in the image of God he created him;
    male and female he created them.

God blessed them, saying:
    "Be fertile and multiply;
    fill the earth and subdue it.
Have dominion over the fish of the sea,
    the birds of the air,
    and all the living things that move on the earth."
God looked at everything he had made,
    and he found it very good.
        GENESIS 1:26–28, 31a

REFLECTION

The one I love, whose hand I hold and whose face I touch,
is the very likeness of God.
To be near the one I love
is to be in the presence of God.
Together as man and woman
we are a mirror image of God.
We were made to be like God—
nothing more and nothing less than this.

- When I look at everything God has made and given to me in you, here is what I find to be "very good" about you. What do you find to be "very good" about me?
- What do we find to be "very good" about us?

PRAYER

For peace in the world, for our families and friends, and for the needs we name this day . . .

God, creator of heaven and earth,
you have revealed yourself in so many ways,
and now you make yourself known in the love we share.
Help us to find and treasure your presence in our love.
Help us to see how we are meant to be your image
not only for each other, but for all who know us.

Our Father . . .

To a long life and a happy life!

It is important to know some background to this story. The book of Tobit in the Bible narrates how Sarah's previous weddings—seven of them—each ended in the death of the groom.

O N their wedding night Tobiah arose from bed and said to
his wife,
"Sister, get up. Let us pray and beg our Lord
to have mercy on us and to grant us deliverance."
Sarah got up, and they started to pray
and beg that deliverance might be theirs.
They began with these words:

"Blessed are you, O God of our fathers;
praised be your name forever and ever.
Let the heavens and all your creation
praise you forever.
You made Adam and you gave him his wife Eve
to be his help and support;
and from these two the human race descended.
You said, 'It is not good for the man to be alone;
let us make him a partner like himself.'
Now, Lord, you know that I take this wife
of mine
not because of lust,
but for a noble purpose.
Call down your mercy on me and on her,
and allow us to live together to a happy
old age."
TOBIT 8:4b–8

REFLECTION

Tobiah and Sarah teach us about trust in God even in the face of life's most difficult circumstances. They had much to fear—death itself—but still, they were ready to praise God and ask for the blessing of a long and happy marriage. Can our faith in God be as strong as theirs?

- What are our concerns and fears about married life?
- Have we brought these concerns and fears to God?
- How do we hope God will bless our marriage?

PRAYER

For the unity of all peoples, for those who have lost hope, and for the needs we name this day . . .

Dear God of our ancestors,
you delivered Sarah and Tobiah from their worst fears.
Help us to come before you
honestly naming our fears and concerns.
Teach us to depend on you and on each other for help.
Give us many years together and help us to grow old
in the shelter of your love.

Our Father . . .

From the Song of Songs

H ARK! my lover—here he comes
   springing across the mountains,
   leaping across the hills.
My lover is like a gazelle
   or a young stag.
Here he stands behind our wall,
   gazing through the windows,
   peering through the lattices.
My lover speaks; he says to me,
   "Arise, my beloved, my dove, my beautiful one, and come!

"O my dove in the clefts of the rock,
   in the secret recesses of the cliff,
Let me see you,
   let me hear your voice,
For your voice is sweet,
   and you are lovely."

My lover belongs to me and I to him.
   He says to me:

"Set me as a seal on your heart,
   as a seal on your arm;
For stern as death is love,
   relentless as the nether-world is devotion;
   its flames are a blazing fire.

Deep waters cannot quench love,
   nor floods sweep it away."
                    SONG OF SONGS 2:8–10, 14, 16a; 8:6–7a

REFLECTION

A solemn truth hides in the poetry and passion of these lyrics,
a truth that is also a promise:
Love is as stern as death.
Marriage is the most awesome commitment we can make.
It is not forever, but it is for life:
for better, for worse, for richer, for poorer,
in sickness and in health, until death shall separate us.
I belong to you, and you to me:
I am yours and you are mine, all the days of my life.

> • To say that I am yours, you are mine, is to entrust ourselves
>   to each other. You make it easy to trust when . . .
> • You make it difficult to trust when . . .

PRAYER

For the work of justice, for the brokenhearted, and for the needs
we name this day . . .

God, the lover of all creation,
help us to trust each other, to trust the love we share.
Let no jealousy come between us.
Calm our fears and make us strong in the love you have given us.

Our Father . . .

A gift, a delight,
and a blessing!

B LESSED the husband of a good wife,
    twice-lengthened are his days;
A worthy wife brings joy to her husband,
    peaceful and full is his life.
A good wife is a generous gift
    bestowed upon him who fears the LORD;
Be he rich or poor, his heart is content,
    and a smile is ever on his face.

A gracious wife delights her husband,
    her thoughtfulness puts flesh on his bones;
A gift from the LORD is her governed speech,
    and her firm virtue is of surpassing worth.
Choicest of blessings is a modest wife,
    priceless her chaste soul.
A holy and decent woman adds grace upon grace;
    indeed, no price is worthy of her temperate soul.
Like the sun rising in the LORD's heavens,
    the beauty of a virtuous wife is the radiance
      of her home.
        SIRACH 26:1–4, 13–16

REFLECTION

Our marriage, the sacrament of living as wife and husband,
will affect our happiness more than anything else.
Our jobs, money, power, position, place of residence—
none of these will bring us greater peace and joy
than our unity and faithfulness as a married couple.
The greatest gift we can give each other
is to promise to be faithful in many, many ways.

- This passage praises a good wife. Could "husband" and "wife" be exchanged in these verses?
- What's my definition of a good husband? A good wife? What are your definitions?
- How did we come by these expectations?
- What people have shown us and taught us what it means to be a good spouse?

PRAYER

For those who have shown us what it means to be a faithful
spouse, and for the needs we name this day . . .

Blessed are you, our God,
both in the heavens and in the homes of your people.
Help us to see in each other your gifts in our lives.
Strengthen us to help each other become good and faithful spouses
that we might share with others the gifts you have given us.

Our Father . . .

God writes a word upon our hearts

T HE days are coming, says the LORD,
    when I will make a new covenant with the
        house of Israel
    and the house of Judah.
It will not be like the covenant I made
        with their fathers:
    the day I took them by the hand
    to lead them forth from the land of Egypt.
But this is the covenant which I will make
    with the house of Israel after those days,
        says the LORD.
I will place my law within them, and write it upon their hearts;
    I will be their God, and they shall be my people.
No longer will they have need to teach their friends and relatives
    how to know the LORD.
All, from least to greatest, shall know me,
        says the LORD.

JEREMIAH 31:31–32a, 33–34a

REFLECTION

These words speak of God's covenant with the chosen people.
The day is coming
when we shall enter into the promise, the covenant, of marriage!
Before God and God's people
we shall promise to love and honor each other
all the days of our lives.
We shall promise to love each other as God loves us—
freely, fully, and faithfully.
The strength and faithfulness of our marriage
is to mirror God's strong and faithful love.
The Lord will be our God,
and we shall be a sign of God's faithfulness
among our friends and families.

- Do others experience our relationship as free and faithful?
- Does our love for each other overflow into the lives of other people?
- What lives are now touched by our love? How?

PRAYER

For the freedom of the oppressed, for those who have been abandoned, and for the needs we name this day . . .

*Dear God, your law is written on our hearts
and we try to follow your ways.
When we fail, your faithfulness and mercy
overshadow our faults and infidelities.
Help us to love fully and freely
and to forgive each other
and those around us.*

Our Father . . .

17

Nothing is more powerful than love

B ROTHERS and sisters:
If God is for us, who can be against us?
He did not spare his own Son
    but handed him over for us all,
      will he not also give us everything else
        along with him?
Who will bring a charge against God's chosen ones?
It is God who acquits us.
Who will condemn?
It is Christ Jesus who died, rather, was raised,
    who also is at the right hand of God,
    who indeed intercedes for us.
What will separate us from the love of Christ?
Will anguish, or distress, or persecution, or famine,
    or nakedness, or peril, or the sword?

No, in all these things, we conquer overwhelmingly
    through him who loved us.
For I am convinced that neither death, nor life,
    nor angels, nor principalities,
    nor present things, nor future things,
    nor powers, nor height, nor depth,
    nor any other creature will be able to separate us
    from the love of God in Christ Jesus our Lord.
ROMANS 8:31b–35, 37–39

REFLECTION

Anguish and distress are part and parcel of a human life
and are sure to be part of our married life.
The scripture tells us that absolutely nothing
can separate us from God's love.
There is no hiding from God's love for us.
Such love is the image of the love we are to share
as husband and wife:
no conditions, no strings attached.

- What have we named as potential "trouble spots" in our marriage?
- Are there any "conditions" we need to let go of?
- Are there any strings that need to be cut?
- Where do we need God's help and love?

PRAYER

For those who suffer distress or hunger, homelessness, or
persecution, and for the needs we name this day . . .

God of life and death, of the heights and the depths,
your love for us is more than we can imagine.
You never stop loving us, even when we sin.
Help us to love each other in ways like this.
Help us to love even when we have been hurt.
Let nothing come between us and your love for us.

Our Father . . .

Sincerely yours

I urge you, brothers and sisters, by the mercies of God,
to offer your bodies as a living sacrifice,
holy and pleasing to God, your spiritual worship.
Do not conform yourselves to this age
but be transformed by the renewal of your mind,
that you may discern what is the will of God,
what is good and pleasing and perfect.

Let love be sincere;
hate what is evil,
hold on to what is good;
love one another with mutual affection;
anticipate one another in showing honor.
Do not grow slack in zeal,
be fervent in spirit,
serve the Lord.
Rejoice in hope,
endure in affliction,
persevere in prayer.
Contribute to the needs of the holy ones,
exercise hospitality.
Bless those who persecute you,
bless and do not curse them.
Rejoice with those who rejoice,
weep with those who weep.

Have the same regard for one another;
   do not be haughty but associate with the lowly;
   do not be wise in your own estimation.
Do not repay anyone evil for evil;
   be concerned for what is noble in the sight of all.
If possible, on your part, live at peace with all.

ROMANS 12:1–2, 9–18

REFLECTION

We spend much time thinking about our relationship.
But our love is not just for ourselves.
Like all love that comes from God,
it is given to us so that we might share it with others.
This passage describes what our married love should be:
good, pleasing, perfect, and sincere.

- Find all of the little "commandments" in this passage.
  How do you and I respond to each of these?
- How do we reach out to those in need? What more could we do?
- Outside of our relationship, how do we live these words?

PRAYER

For the poor and prisoners, for those who mourn, and for the needs
we name this day . . .

God, you rejoice with our rejoicing,
   you weep with our weeping.
Help us to be always looking out for others' needs,
   sharing what you have given us.
Help us to hold on to what is good,
   to live peaceably with everyone,
   to have the same regard for all.

Our Father . . .

The beauty of your body

BROTHERS and sisters:
The body is not for immorality, but for the Lord,
and the Lord is for the body;
God raised the Lord and will also raise us
by his power.

Do you not know that your bodies are members of Christ?
Whoever is joined to the Lord becomes one spirit with him.
Avoid immorality.
Every other sin a person commits is outside the body,
but the immoral person sins against his own body.
Do you not know that your body
is a temple of the Holy Spirit within you,
whom you have from God, and that you are not your own?
For you have been purchased at a price.
Therefore glorify God in your body.

1 CORINTHIANS 6:13c–15a, 17–20

REFLECTION

The beauty I see in your body, the beauty you see in mine,
is a gift from God.
What we find attractive about each other
draws us together and makes us long to be one flesh.
The Spirit of God is not absent from our flesh and our longing.
We are meant to honor and respect our bodies
as gifts of God and temples of the Holy Spirit.

- Do we understand that God's gift of love to us includes our sexual desire for each other?
- Do we believe that our desire to hold and touch each other, and our desire to make love as husband and wife, is God's gift to us?
- How can we help each other to honor our sexuality?

PRAYER

For those who are lonely, and for the needs we name this day . . .

God, your glory is proclaimed
in body and in spirit,
in the desire we have for one another—
great, strong, and wonderful.
Sometimes this desire is our comfort,
and sometimes it is overwhelming.
Help us to be gentle in learning to love and hold each other.
Help each of us to remember:
I am not my own—I am yours.
And we are God's.

Our Father . . .

Without love, we are nothing

B ROTHERS and sisters:
Strive eagerly for the greatest spiritual gifts.

But I shall show you a still more excellent way.

If I speak in human and angelic tongues
    but do not have love,
    I am a resounding gong or a clashing cymbal.
And if I have the gift of prophecy
    and comprehend all mysteries and all knowledge;
    if I have all faith so as to move mountains,
    but do not have love, I am nothing.
If I give away everything I own,
    and if I hand my body over so that I may boast
    but do not have love, I gain nothing.

Love is patient, love is kind.
It is not jealous, is not pompous,
    it is not inflated, it is not rude,
    it does not seek its own interests,
    it is not quick-tempered, it does not brood over injury,
        it does not rejoice over wrongdoing
    but rejoices with the truth.
It bears all things, believes all things,
    hopes all things, endures all things.
Love never fails.
       1 CORINTHIANS 12:31—13:8a

REFLECTION

These words capture our attention and imagination!
They describe the love that God expects of us.
Poems and lyrics hint at such love;
this greatest of all gifts comes alive in people,
in the deeds we do and in the sacrifices we make.
The scripture's description of love
should be a description of us.

- Beginning with the line "Love is patient . . ." we'll insert our names in place of the word *love*. How does our relationship come to life in these beautiful words?
- Is our relationship true to this description?
- Where do we need to grow?

PRAYER

For peace among nations, for those whose hearts have grown cold,
and for the needs we name this day . . .

God, you have loved us beyond our knowing.
Teach us how to love you, our neighbor, ourselves—
without limits.
Help us to see that nothing is stronger
than the love with which you have brought us together,
the love with which you sustain us.

Our Father . . .

New clothes for the wedding and for life

B ROTHERS and sisters:
Put on, as God's chosen ones, holy and beloved,
    heartfelt compassion, kindness, humility, gentleness,
        and patience,
    bearing with one another and forgiving one another,
    if one has a grievance against another;
    as the Lord has forgiven you, so must you also do.
And over all these put on love,
    that is, the bond of perfection.
And let the peace of Christ control your hearts,
    the peace into which you were also called
        in one Body.
And be thankful.
Let the word of Christ dwell in you richly,
    as in all wisdom you teach and admonish one another,
    singing psalms, hymns, and spiritual songs
    with gratitude in your hearts to God.
And whatever you do, in word or in deed,
    do everything in the name of the Lord Jesus,
    giving thanks to God the Father through him.
        COLOSSIANS 3:12–17

REFLECTION

Tuxedos, gowns, veils, colors, flowers!
Special clothes for a joyous and festive day!
But there's another kind of clothing
that will wear better and longer:
heartfelt compassion, kindness, humility, gentleness, and patience.
These are the clothes that will make us truly beautiful,
the clothes that will serve us well, season after season.

- Let's "try on" these clothes mentioned in the reading:
  compassion, kindness, humility, gentleness, patience,
  forgiveness, love, peace, thankfulness. How do they "fit"?
- Does anything need to be "taken in" or "let out"?
- Do we bear with each other?
- Do we forgive each other?
- Are we able to teach and correct one another?

PRAYER

For all who work for justice and for peace, and for the needs we
name this day . . .

Lord God, gently enfolding all in your mercy,
you see only how our hearts are clothed.
Teach us to be patient,
dedicate us to the works of peace,
help us to forgive as freely as you forgive us.
Our hearts are filled with thanksgiving for all we have received.

Our Father . . .

Living and loving, in deed and truth

CHILDREN, let us love not in word or speech
but in deed and truth.

Now this is how we shall know that we belong
to the truth
and reassure our hearts before him
in whatever our hearts condemn,
for God is greater than our hearts and knows everything.
Beloved, if our hearts do not condemn us,
we have confidence in God
and receive from him whatever we ask,
because we keep his commandments and do what pleases him.
And his commandment is this:
we should believe in the name of his Son, Jesus Christ,
and love one another just as he commanded us.
Those who keep his commandments remain
in him, and he in them,
and the way we know that he remains in us
is from the Spirit that he gave us.

1 JOHN 3:18–24

REFLECTION

We love to be told that we are loved,
but words of love alone do not suffice.
We also love to be *shown* that we are loved.
Jesus is God's Word, God's love become a deed.
Our words of love must also become deeds of love:
This is how love comes alive and flourishes.
Words of love are important;
we need to speak them and hear them,
but words alone are not enough.
Love must live in deeds if it is to live in truth.

- When do we tell each other of our love? Is Valentine's Day or a wedding anniversary enough?
- When do we tell our family and friends of our love for them?
- How do we show each other, and others, our love?

PRAYER

For all God's children, for all who seek the truth, and for the needs we name this day . . .

God of truth, greater than our hearts,
your love for us is told in every new moment,
told in the lives of all good people,
told most simply in the cross of Jesus.
Help us speak the love in our hearts,
in words and in deeds, day after day in good times and bad.

Our Father . . .

This is what love means

Beloved, let us love one another,
because love is of God;
everyone who loves is begotten by God
and knows God.
Whoever is without love does not know God,
for God is love.
In this way the love of God was revealed to us:
God sent his only-begotten Son into the world
so that we might have life through him.
In this is love:
not that we have loved God, but that he loved us
and sent his Son as expiation for our sins.
Beloved, if God so loved us,
we also must love one another.
No one has ever seen God.
Yet, if we love one another, God remains in us,
and his love is brought to perfection in us.

1 JOHN 4:7–12

REFLECTION

The word *love* appears fourteen times in these five verses!
Does the word *love* say it all?
The love we have for each other
is sometimes more than words can speak.
Often it is only in sharing silence
that we communicate what we know and feel.
God's love for us was more than words could speak:
The word became flesh, to live among us.

- What does it mean that we should "love one another"? What has our love for one another to do with God's love for all?
- What words fill out the meaning of our word *love*?
- What words fill out the meaning of our word *sin*?

PRAYER

For those who do not know God, for those who do not know love,
and for the needs we name this day . . .

Blessed are you, Lord God of all creation,
for you open our eyes, our hearts, and our minds
to your presence in our love and in our world.
Do we ever see and hear and know how close you are to us?
Help us to open our arms to all
who are in need of the love you have given us,
thus bring your love to perfection in us.

Our Father . . .

Party time!

I, John, heard what sounded like the loud voice
of a great multitude in heaven, saying:

"Alleluia!
Salvation, glory, and might belong to our God."

A voice coming from the throne said:

"Praise our God, all you his servants,
and you who revere him, small and great."

Then I heard something like the sound
of a great multitude
or the sound of rushing water or mighty peals of thunder,
as they said:
"Alleluia!
The Lord has established his reign,
our God, the almighty.
Let us rejoice and be glad
and give him glory.
For the wedding day of the Lamb has come,
his bride has made herself ready.
She was allowed to wear
a bright, clean linen garment."
(The linen represents the righteous deeds of the holy ones.)

Then the angel said to me,
 "Write this:
 Blessed are those who have been called
 to the wedding feast of the Lamb."
REVELATION 19:1, 5–9a

REFLECTION

The wedding day in the book of Revelation
sounds like a great party that goes on forever!
We hope that our wedding reception
will be a time of reunion and rejoicing.
God's kingdom is like a marriage feast
to which the small and the great are all invited.
Our marriage is meant to open our hearts, like God's heart,
to welcome our children and all who may come to us in need.

- As we prepare our own wedding day, how can we make an offering to those who have no feasting, no food?
- Do we need to make peace with someone invited to our wedding?
- As a married couple, how will we respond to those in need?
- How are we approaching the gift-giving that will happen with our wedding?

PRAYER

For the poor of the world, for our wedding guests, and for the needs we name this day . . .

God of the great wedding day,
you are our lover, our spouse, forever.
As the day of our own rejoicing approaches,
help us to give careful attention to the liturgy at the church,
gracious hospitality to our guests at the party afterward,
and a share of all we have to those who are in need.

Our Father . . .

Be glad!

WHEN Jesus saw the crowds, he went up
the mountain,
and after he had sat down, his disciples came to him.
He began to teach them, saying:

"Blessed are the poor in spirit,
for theirs is the Kingdom of heaven.
Blessed are they who mourn,
for they will be comforted.
Blessed are the meek,
for they will inherit the land.
Blessed are they who hunger and thirst
for righteousness,
for they will be satisfied.
Blessed are the merciful,
for they will be shown mercy.
Blessed are the clean of heart,
for they will see God.
Blessed are the peacemakers,
for they will be called children of God.
Blessed are they who are persecuted for the
sake of righteousness,
for theirs is the Kingdom of heaven.

Blessed are you when they insult you and persecute you
and utter every kind of evil against you
falsely because of me.
Rejoice and be glad,
for your reward will be great in heaven."

MATTHEW 5:1–12a

REFLECTION

These words echo with beauty and strength;
these words ask us to look again,
and to look yet again.
Every line here turns upside down our ideas
about happiness and success.
The Lord asks us to wonder about what really makes us happy
and to see a path that leads to life and peace and rejoicing.

- What do you and I think will make us happy?
- What would we call success in our marriage?
- Who are "they" in each of these scripture verses?
- How would we come to be numbered among those who are "glad and rejoice"?
- How have we dealt with suffering?

PRAYER

For exiles and refugees, for political prisoners and all prisoners, and
for the needs we name this day . . .

God, your blessing rests where the world least expects.
Help us to be hungry and thirsty for what is good and holy,
to be merciful makers of peace,
to be ever attentive to the persecuted and oppressed.
For then shall we be glad and rejoice.

Our Father . . .

Going public with our love

J ESUS said to his disciples:
"You are the salt of the earth.
But if salt loses its taste, with what
        can it be seasoned?
It is no longer good for anything
    but to be thrown out and trampled underfoot.
You are the light of the world.
A city set on a mountain cannot be hidden.
Nor do they light a lamp and then put it
        under a bushel basket;
    it is set on a lamp stand,
    where it gives light to all in the house.
Just so, your light must shine before others,
    that they may see your good deeds
    and glorify your heavenly Father."
                MATTHEW 5:13–16

REFLECTION

As personal and intimate a decision as marriage is,
it is also a very public affair,
the business of a community.
The scriptures keep urging us to move beyond ourselves
to the needs of others,
sharing what we have received from God in love.
Others should be able to count on us,
to look to us for love, for fidelity,
to see the light, and to taste the salt of God's presence
in our community.

- Does our relationship invite others in or keep them at a distance?
- What kind of example do we offer to single friends? To married friends? To our families?
- What do we want them to see?
- What do they see?

PRAYER

For those who have no eagerness for life, for those who reveal the light of truth, and for the needs we name this day . . .

Lord Jesus,
in the simple gifts of creation
you found images to tell us of our calling.
We seek the light that shines
in all the good people we have known.
Help us become light for others.
We seek the saltiness that enlivens human community.
Help us become salt of the earth
as we pray to the Father in the words you gave us:

Our Father . . .

It did not collapse

J ESUS said to his disciples:
"Not everyone who says to me, 'Lord, Lord,'
will enter the Kingdom of heaven,
but only the one who does the will
of my Father in heaven.

"Everyone who listens to these words of mine and acts on them
will be like a wise man who built his house on rock.
The rain fell, the floods came,
and the winds blew and buffeted the house.
But it did not collapse;
it had been set solidly on rock.
And everyone who listens to these words of mine
but does not act on them
will be like a fool who built his house on sand.
The rain fell, the floods came,
and the winds blew and buffeted the house.
And it collapsed and was completely ruined."

When Jesus finished these words,
the crowds were astonished at his teaching,
for he taught them as one having authority,
and not as their scribes.

MATTHEW 7:21, 24–29

REFLECTION

Our marriage will survive:
so we trust, hope, and pray.
We need to build the home of our love
on something greater than our own strengths and resources.
We need the help of God
and we need good friends all the days of our lives.
We need to build our marriage
on the rock of faithful love.

- What is the foundation of our relationship now?
- What happens when the storms come along?
- What happens when one of us is the storm?
- Where do we turn when our own strengths are not enough?
- Do we know other couples whose foundation is their faith in God and their membership in the church?
- How have we seen their faith come to life?

PRAYER

For wives and husbands, the young and the old, and for the needs
we name this day . . .

God of calm and of storm,
we want to be filled with faith in each other
all the days of our lives.
Teach us to depend on you as we depend on each other.
Then we shall build our home
on the rock of your love,
and there shall all people be welcome.

Our Father . . .

Let no one separate

S OME Pharisees approached Jesus,
  and tested him, saying,
 "Is it lawful for a man to divorce his wife
  for any cause whatever?"
He said in reply, "Have you not read that from the beginning
 the Creator *made them male and female* and said,
 For this reason a man shall leave his father and mother
 and be joined to his wife, and the two shall become one flesh?
So they are no longer two, but one flesh.
Therefore, what God has joined together,
  man must not separate."
   MATTHEW 19:3–6

REFLECTION

We both have friends and family members
who have been divorced.
We have seen marriages break apart.
Some of these people will celebrate our wedding with us.
Our hearts go out to them and to their children.
And our hearts hope for the strength and grace we need
to enter into so great a covenant as marriage.

- What makes us think we'll beat the divorce statistics?
- What changes have we learned to accept in each other?
- Are we ready for a lifetime of living with changes?
- How do we think we will be in ten years?

PRAYER

For those who strive to build communities that support women
and men in married life, and for the needs we name this day . . .

God of our separateness and our union,
we shall promise to share a life and home
until death parts us.
Give us strength and love to keep such vows.
Let no one separate what you join in us.

Our Father . . .

Loving with everything you've got

ONE of the Pharisees, a scholar of the law,
   tested Jesus by asking,
"Teacher, which commandment in the law
   is the greatest?"
He said to him,
"You shall love the Lord, your God,
   with all your heart,
   with all your soul,
   and with all your mind.
This is the greatest and the first commandment.
The second is like it:
   You shall love your neighbor as yourself.
The whole law and the prophets depend
   on these two commandments."

MATTHEW 22:35–40

REFLECTION

It sounds like the Lord wants *everything:*
our hearts, our souls, our minds!
No one has a greater claim on our lives and our love
than the God who made us.
And after God comes the neighbor.
That is the sum of it.
That is the foundation of all we have to do,
of all we have to teach our children.

- God's claim on my life and my love is greater than yours, and faithfully loving you is the first way I can serve God as a married person. Can I say that and believe it and mean it?
- Is our praying together helping us to become more aware of God in our relationship and in our future?

PRAYER

For the unity of the church, for those who serve the poor, and for the needs we name this day . . .

Lord our God,
you command every kind of love we can give.
In giving of ourselves to you
we lose nothing and gain everything.
In serving others,
make us faithful stewards of what you have given us.

Our Father . . .

The Lord is a wedding guest

T HERE was a wedding in Cana in Galilee,
    and the mother of Jesus was there.
Jesus and his disciples were also invited
        to the wedding.
When the wine ran short,
    the mother of Jesus said to him,
    "They have no wine."
And Jesus said to her,
    "Woman, how does your concern affect me?
My hour has not yet come."
His mother said to the servers,
    "Do whatever he tells you."
Now there were six stone water jars there
        for Jewish ceremonial washings,
    each holding twenty to thirty gallons.
Jesus told them,
    "Fill the jars with water."
So they filled them to the brim.
Then he told them,
    "Draw some out now and take it
        to the headwaiter."
So they took it.
And when the headwaiter tasted the water
        that had become wine,

without knowing where it came from
(although the servants who had drawn the water knew),
the headwaiter called the bridegroom and said to him,
"Everyone serves good wine first,
and then when people have drunk freely, an inferior one;
but you have kept the good wine until now."
Jesus did this as the beginning of his signs in Cana in Galilee
and so revealed his glory,
and his disciples began to believe in him.

JOHN 2:1–11

REFLECTION

Can you imagine how happy Jesus was for this couple?
Just so, the Lord loves us!
There may not be any dazzling miracles at our wedding reception,
but he is ready to be with us in our times of need, now and always.

- The Lord took what the couple already had, just water, and turned it into the finest wine. What needs to be transformed in our lives? In our relationship?
- When do we ask the Lord for help?

PRAYER

For all married couples, for those preparing for marriage, and for
the needs we name this day . . .

God of all our rejoicing,
Jesus revealed his glory at the wedding in Cana,
glory in the abundance of wine and delight.
We invite your Son into our marriage,
and we thirst for the choice wine of joy and patience.
May we be ever open to the guests you send us.

Our Father . . .

So that your joy may be complete

J ESUS said to his disciples:
"As the Father loves me, so I also love you.
Remain in my love.
If you keep my commandments, you will remain in my love,
    just as I have kept my Father's commandments
    and remain in his love.

"I have told you this so that my joy might be in you
    and your joy might be complete.
This is my commandment: love one another
    as I love you."

      JOHN 15:9–12

REFLECTION

These words are not addressed to individual engaged couples,
not even to married couples—but to the whole church!
The people who proclaim and try to live this message
are the church.
"Complete joy" is not something you and I will find by ourselves:
It is the joy of sharing with others who believe as we do.
It is the support of other believers
that helps us to love as deeply as these words command.

- What's our relationship with the church now?
- Has our preparation for marriage helped us grow closer
  to the church?
- Do we have questions about the church? Have we tried to have
  them answered?
- What do we have to offer a parish community?
- Where will we worship on Sundays after our wedding?

PRAYER

For those who have forgotten joy, for those who daily lay down
their lives out of love, and for the needs we name this day . . .

God of wondrous love,
love is your command and love is your gift to us.
This love embraced us when we were baptized in the death
and the resurrection of Jesus.
Show us what it means that he called us friends.
Teach us to ponder and keep his commandments.

Our Father . . .

THE RITE OF MARRIAGE

E ACH of the following units begins with a text from the Rite of Marriage of the Roman Catholic Church. These texts include prayers, instructions, intercessions, blessings, and the marriage vows. These are the words that will shape your wedding liturgy. Praying with these words now will help you to pray with them on your wedding day. Let all of them touch you deeply, and learn at least some of them by heart—always including your marriage vows.

The opening prayer

F ATHER,
you have made the bond of marriage
a holy mystery,
a symbol of Christ's love for his Church.
Hear our prayers for _____ and _____ .
With faith in you and in each other
they pledge their love today.
May their lives always bear witness
to the reality of that love.

REFLECTION

On that day, at that moment, and in that place
when we will speak the most important words of our lives,
our families and friends will be gathered around us, praying for us,
praying that we will be faithful to the vows we speak
and that God will be faithful to us.
What a wonderful gift to receive:
the heartfelt prayers of those who love us!

- Who are we inviting to pray with us on our wedding day?
- How will we welcome them to our celebration?
- How will we provide for their participation in prayers
  and songs?
- For whom should we be praying now?

PRAYER

For those most in need of prayer, for those who pray for us, and for
the needs we name this day . . .

Faithful God of hard promises,
hear our prayers for those who have loved us,
especially our families and friends.
Hear their prayers for us, now and on our wedding day,
so that with faith in you and in each other
we may pledge our love and so be living witnesses
to your love for all creation.

Our Father . . .

Promising in the presence of the church

The presider will address us with these words:

M Y dear friends,
you have come together in this church
so that the Lord may seal and strengthen your love
in the presence of the Church's minister
and this community.
Christ abundantly blesses this love.
He has already consecrated you in baptism
and now he enriches and strengthens you
by a special sacrament
so that you may assume the duties of marriage
in mutual and lasting fidelity.
And so, in the presence of the Church,
I ask you to state your intentions.
_____ and _____ ,
have you come here freely and without reservation
to give yourselves to each other in marriage?
Will you love and honor each other as man and wife
for the rest of your lives?
Will you accept children lovingly from God and bring them up
according to the law of Christ and his Church?

REFLECTION

With these words, everything is on the line!
We have come here to celebrate a sacrament
that will bind us together until death separates us.
We come here with no holding back in our minds and hearts.
We come here freely, filled with hope and promise
that our fidelity will be mutual and lasting.
We promise to allow our love to give birth to new life,
and we promise to raise our children
according to the gospel of Jesus.

> • These solemn words are deserving of our full attention.
> The more deeply we ponder them now, the more filled with
> meaning they will be for us on our wedding day. We'll
> take turns reading aloud to each other the address and the
> questions, listening carefully to the words and carefully
> considering our answers.

PRAYER

For single parents, for orphans and abandoned children, and for
the needs we name this day . . .

> *God, the seal and strength of all love,*
> *help us to give of ourselves without reservation.*
> *Lift up our hearts in thanksgiving*
> *that we might accept the responsibilities and challenges*
> *of married life.*
>
> *Our Father . . .*

The exchange of vows

The presider will address us with these words:

Since it is your intention to enter into marriage,
join your right hands,
and declare your consent before God and his Church.

REFLECTION

As we prepare to speak words that change our lives,
it will be a comfort and a source of strength
to hold each other's hand.
With this simple gesture,
in the presence of God
and the company of families and friends,
we will declare our intention
to enter into this most sacred union.
Once we have exchanged our vows,
the church will look to us and count on us
to be living signs of God's faithful love.

- At what moments does my hand reach out to you or your hand to me?
- What does this gesture mean to us?
- We will begin our married life in church, at the Lord's altar. How will it feel to be a "married couple" within our parish?

PRAYER

For our parents and grandparents and for all who have taken
our hands in love and protection, and for the needs we name
this day . . .

Dear God,
we join our hands even now. . . .
Be with those who have no one to take their hand.
Remember in mercy those who have held our hands over the years.
Hold us in the palm of your hand.
With hands joined,
we pray in the words our Savior gave us:

Our Father . . .

he VOWS

The marriage vows are exchanged using one of these two forms:

I, _____ , take you, _____ , to be my wife.
I promise to be true to you in good times and in bad,
in sickness and in health.
I will love you and honor you
all the days of my life.

I, _____ , take you, _____ , to be my husband.
I promise to be true to you in good times and in bad,
in sickness and in health.
I will love you and honor you
all the days of my life.

　　Or:

I, _____ , take you, _____ , for my lawful husband,
to have and to hold, from this day forward,
for better, for worse,
for richer, for poorer,
in sickness and in health,
until death do us part.

I, _____ , take you, _____ , for my lawful wife,
to have and to hold, from this day forward,
for better, for worse,
for richer, for poorer,
in sickness and in health,
until death do us part.

REFLECTION

Like the Lord's Prayer, like the lyrics of "our" song,
let these words be engraved on our hearts and minds.
We need to say them and pray them often—
so often that they become a part of us,
so often that we know them by heart.
These are not words for just one day;
they are words for a lifetime.
No words will ever speak more fully
the love that is ours to give and receive.

> • Which of the two texts "says it best" for us?
> • What do these words ask of me?
> • What does it mean that someone speaks these words to me?
> • Let's write our names in the blanks and learn these words
>   by heart.

PRAYER

For those who have been betrayed, for those who struggle to be
faithful, and for the needs we name this day . . .

> *Blessed are you, God of all creation.*
> *With all the simplicity of words,*
> *with all the strength of words,*
> *we two shall wed each other.*
> *May your own word be in our speaking,*
> *your promise in our vows,*
> *your blessing in our union.*
>
> *Our Father . . .*

What God has joined together

After the exchange of vows, the presider proclaims:

Y OU have declared your consent before the Church.
May the Lord in his goodness strengthen your consent
   and fill you both with his blessings.
What God has joined,
   men must not divide.

REFLECTION

In the midst of the gathered church,
in the name of the church,
we are here called married.
No one must separate what God has joined:
We are joined in marriage
and even a lifetime will not be long enough
to unfold that mystery.

- Are we ready to ask God to do something in our lives that no one can undo?
- Are we making vows without any reservation?
- Are we ready to ask the church to stand as a witness to our promise to be faithful until death parts us?
- Is this witness what we are really asking of those who are to be our attendants and of all those present?

PRAYER

For our parents, brothers and sisters, for all who bring God's love to others, and for the needs we name this day . . .

God of all comfort,
our love for each other is strong
but sometimes we are weak.
Let your goodness be our strength.
Let nothing divide what you have brought together.

Our Father . . .

Exchange of rings

The presider prays in these words:

L ORD,
bless and consecrate _____ and _____
in their love for each other.
May these rings be a symbol
of true faith in each other
and always remind them of their love.

We say:

_____ , take this ring as a sign of my love and fidelity. In the
name of the Father, and of the Son, and of the Holy Spirit.

REFLECTION

The church does not require the exchange or wearing of rings.
For many years only one ring was given, the bride's.
Today's usual practice involves a *mutual* exchange of rings
as signs of promised faithfulness.
In this prayer, the presider blesses not the rings, but us.
The giving of the rings proclaims:
Wear this as a sign for all to see:
not a sign that you belong to me,
but a sign that I am faithful to you in all things.
Without our even knowing it,
strangers will identify us as married persons.
Even when we are apart from each other,
our rings will remind us of the love we have promised.

- How are the rings like other gifts we have given each other?
- How are they unique?
- Why does a ring have this association with marriage?
- Do we have other traditions in our families or ethnic backgrounds of similar meaning and importance?

PRAYER

For all who need to extend and receive forgiveness, and for the needs we name this day . . .

God of Abraham and Sarah, Rebekah and Isaac,
our rings will mark us as married people.
Let no thought or deed of ours betray the fidelity
that our rings will signify.

Our Father . . .

61

The general intercessions

The general intercessions or "prayer of the faithful" follows the exchange of rings. The prayers found here are examples.

F OR justice to be done and for peaceful times,
let us pray to the Lord.

For the church throughout the world,
for all gathered here
and for those who could not be here with us,
let us pray to the Lord.

For the poor and all the oppressed,
for the sick and the dying,
let us pray to the Lord.

For all households,
for the young and the old,
for the spirit of kindness and compassion,
let us pray to the Lord.

For _____ , and _____ , who marry this day,
let us pray to the Lord.

For all who have died,
especially for _____ ,
let us pray to the Lord.

REFLECTION

These petitions sweep the whole world
and draw our attention and our prayer to the needs of others.
Our wedding will be a time for us to remember:
Even in the midst of our joy,
we stand before God with all the needy of the world.
Our married life, too,
should draw our attention, our prayer, our resources, and our work
to the needs of those whose lives are heavily burdened.

PRAYER

Pray the intercessions together and conclude with the Lord's Prayer.

From the eucharistic prayer

If the eucharist is celebrated at the wedding,
the presider leads all in this prayer.

T HE Lord be with you.
  And also with you.
Lift up your hearts.
  We lift them up to the Lord.
Let us give thanks to the Lord our God.
  It is right to give him thanks and praise.

Father, all-powerful and ever-living God,
we do well always and everywhere to give you thanks.
By this sacrament your grace unites man and woman
in an unbreakable bond of love and peace.

You have designed the chaste love of husband and wife
for the increase both of the human family
and of your own family born in baptism.

You are the loving Father of the world of nature;
you are the loving Father of the new creation of grace.
In Christian marriage you bring together the two orders
     of creation:
nature's gift of children enriches the world
and your grace enriches also your Church.

Through Christ the choirs of angels
and all the saints
praise and worship your glory.

REFLECTION

Few things in today's world are "unbreakable,"
but that's exactly the word used to describe
the bond of our love as husband and wife.
So strong is our love meant to be
that the church and the whole world
are enriched by what God joins together in our lives.
The church and the world are also increased and enriched
by the children who may be born of our love.

- We begin the church's eucharistic prayer by saying that we will lift our hearts and give thanks and praise to God. The prayer praises God for the marriage bond; it will go on to give thanks for Jesus and the work of our redemption. How can this lifting of hearts and our own prayers of praise be part of each day for us individually and as a couple?
- How will we pray before we share a meal together?

PRAYER

For the whole church, singing God's praise, and for the needs we name this day . . .

Holy God,
in good times and bad,
bring us together each Sunday
around that table
where we join with sisters and brothers
to give you thanks and praise.

Our Father . . .

From a nuptial blessing

The presider prays in these words:

F ATHER, keep them always true to your commandments.
Keep them faithful in marriage
and let them be living examples of Christian life.
Give them the strength which comes from the gospel
so that they may be witnesses of Christ to others.
Bless them with children
and help them to be good parents.
May they live to see their children's children.
And after a happy old age,
grant them fullness of life with the saints
in the kingdom of heaven.

REFLECTION

These words are a blessing.
With such blessings,
Jews and Christians pray that God's gifts
abound in our homes, our lives.
Little by little we will work out this blessing,
renew it, give it to others,
and so come to its fullness.

- When do we "bless ourselves"?
- When have we been blessed by another?
- Will we be comfortable asking God's blessing at mealtime and at bedtime?
- When the time comes to bless our child, each night before sleep, how will we do this? What words and gestures will we use?

PRAYER

For the people of our diocese and of our parish, and for the needs we name this day . . .

Blessed are you, Lord God of all creation,
in our parents and ancestors,
in our children and our children's children,
and in each other.

Our Father . . .

Prayer after communion

If the eucharist is celebrated, the presider prays these words after communion:

L ORD,
we who have shared the food of your table
pray for our friends _____ and _____ ,
whom you have joined together in marriage.
Keep them close to you always.
May their love for each other
proclaim to all the world
their faith in you.

REFLECTION

We are one in faith, one in baptism,
one in the Lord.
This is what we show each Sunday
when we eat the one bread
and drink the cup of salvation.
Soon we will be one in the sacrament of marriage,
ourselves an image of the love of God for creation.

- Do we come to the eucharist together?
- Do we have a better understanding as we get older of what it means to say "Amen" when the minister of communion says, "The body of Christ," "The blood of Christ"?
- How will we make the table in our new home a place to share together and to pray together?

PRAYER

For the people we pray with on Sundays, and for the needs we name this day . . .

Jesus, lamb of God,
bread of heaven and cup of our salvation,
we become one with you in your church.
Make strong our unity with each other and with you.
Let nothing separate us from your love.
Teach us again to pray:

Our Father . . .

A blessing of the bride and groom

MAY almighty God, with his Word of blessing, unite your hearts in the never-ending bond of pure love.
Amen.

May your children bring you happiness and may your generous love for them be returned to you many times over.
Amen.

May the peace of Christ live always in your hearts and
in your home.
May you have true friends to stand by you, both in joy and
in sorrow.
May you be ready and willing to help and comfort all who come
to you in need.
And may the blessings promised to the compassionate be yours
in abundance.
Amen.

May you find happiness and satisfaction in your work.
May daily problems never cause you undue anxiety, nor the desire
for earthly possessions dominate your lives.
But may your hearts' first desire always be the good things waiting
for you in the life of heaven.
Amen.

May the Lord bless you with many happy years together, so that
you may enjoy the rewards of a good life.

And after you have served him loyally in his kingdom on earth,
    may he welcome you to his eternal kingdom in heaven.
    Amen.

And may almighty God bless you all,
the Father, and the Son, and the Holy Spirit.
    Amen.

REFLECTION

This blessing is lengthy, but it covers just about everything,
right up to eternity with the Lord in heaven!
There are so many ways in which we need God's blessing
on our lives, our love, our home, our families, our future.
May our families and friends and all present
extend their blessing to us as this is prayed upon our marriage.

> • Which lines of this blessing invite some reflection?
> • What do we know about "true friends"?
> • Are we ready to comfort others "in need"?
> • What anxiety does either of us have? Is it "undue"?
> • We'll take turns now praying over each of the different sections
>   of this blessing . . .

PRAYER

For the spirit of joy and of peace in our lives, and for the needs we
name this day . . .

> *God, the source of all blessing,*
> *together we come to you*
> *and ask for your amazing grace:*
> *good friends, the spirit of compassion,*
> *joy in our children, hearts set on what matters.*
> *Make us be a blessing to others:*
> *to our families, our children, strangers, and friends.*

> *Our Father . . .*

71

The dismissal

G O in peace to love and serve the Lord.
Thanks be to God.

REFLECTION

We will leave the church to go to our reception,
and then on to our wedding trip.
But we will be leaving the church
joined in a way we had not been when we entered.
We will leave the church building, blessed by God's grace,
that we might be the church,
a sign of God's love "all the days of our lives."

- When all the festivities are over and we have returned from
  our trip, how will "to love and serve the Lord" be the direction
  of our lives?
- Sunday worship and church involvement will be an important
  part of this. What else?

PRAYER

For those who are peacemakers in every community, and for the
needs we name this day . . .

God of all our days and nights,
the wedding we look forward to will last a day;
the marriage we enter will be for a lifetime.
Send us in peace and love to serve you
by loving each other
and by sharing that love with all the people we know
and with those in need.

Our Father . . .

OTHER PRAYERS AND BLESSINGS

T HIS section contains a number of prayers.
Some of them you already will know by heart.
At times, one of these prayers would be appropriate
at the conclusion of your times of prayer together.

Also included are two prayer services for use at
home with your families and friends. One is a blessing
for a couple upon their becoming engaged; the other
is a blessing for a son or daughter, just prior to the
celebration of the marriage. These are opportunities
to invite your friends and families to pray with you.

All of these texts are taken from *Catholic Household
Blessings and Prayers*. This is a book intended by
the United States bishops for every Catholic home.
It contains prayers for meals, for the seasons and
feasts, and for the great and small events of family
life. Be sure that a good translation of the Bible
and a copy of *Catholic Household Blessings and Prayers*
are among the essentials for your new home.

Prayers

INTERCESSIONS

Let us pray to God who cares for all, and with earnest humility say:
R. Have mercy on your people, Lord.

Guard the Church.
Watch over N., our Pope.
Protect and bless N., our bishop.
Save your people.
Preserve peace among nations.
Bring an end to strife and hatred.
Guide the rulers of the nations.
Guide parents in the fulfillment of their responsibilities.
Nourish children by your loving care.
Support and give solace to the aged.
Be a helper to the poor.
Comfort those who are troubled.
Grant deliverance to captives.
Bring exiles back to their homeland.
Grant health to the sick.
Be present to those who are dying.
Admit those who have died into the company of the saints.

THE LITURGY OF THE HOURS

HAIL MARY

Hail Mary, full of grace,
the Lord is with you!
Blessed are you among women,
and blessed is the fruit of your womb, Jesus.
Holy Mary, Mother of God,
pray for us sinners,
now and at the hour of our death.
Amen.

MORNING PRAYERS

Upon waking, make the sign of the cross and say:

In the name of the Father, and of the Son, and of the Holy Spirit.
Amen.

Or trace a small cross on the lips and say:

Lord, open my lips,
and my mouth will proclaim your praise.

Glory to the Father, and to the Son, and to the Holy Spirit:
as it was in the beginning, is now, and will be for ever.

MEAL PRAYERS

BEFORE EATING AND DRINKING
Bless us, O Lord, and these your gifts
which we are about to receive from your goodness.
Through Christ our Lord.
Amen.

AFTER EATING AND DRINKING
We give you thanks for all your gifts, almighty God,
living and reigning now and for ever.
Amen.

NIGHT PRAYERS

May the all-powerful Lord grant us a restful night
and a peaceful death.

Protect us, Lord, as we stay awake;
watch over us as we sleep,
that awake, we may keep watch with Christ,
and asleep, rest in his peace.

I confess to almighty God,
and to you, my brothers and sisters,
that I have sinned through my own fault
in my thoughts and in my words,
in what I have done,
and in what I have failed to do;
and I ask blessed Mary, ever virgin,
all the angels and saints,
and you, my brothers and sisters,
to pray for me to the Lord our God.

Visit this house,
we beg you, Lord,
and banish from it
the deadly power of the evil one.
May your holy angels dwell here
to keep us in peace,
and may your blessing be always upon us.
We ask this through Christ our Lord.
Amen.

Blessings

BLESSING OF AN ENGAGED COUPLE

Ordinarily, the blessing of an engaged couple is celebrated by both families, perhaps at a meal together.

All make the sign of the cross. One of the parents begins:

Brothers and sisters,
let us praise our Lord Jesus Christ,
who loved us and gave himself for us.
Let us bless him now and for ever.

All respond:

Blessed be God for ever.

The leader may use these or similar words to introduce the blessing:

We know that all of us need God's blessing at all times; but at the time of their engagement to be married, Christians are in particular need of grace as they prepare themselves to form a new family.

Let us pray, then, for God's blessing to come upon this couple, our brother and sister: that as they await the day of their wedding, they will grow in mutual respect and in their love for one another; that through their companionship and prayer together they will prepare themselves rightly and chastely for marriage.

Then the scripture is read:

Listen to the words of the apostle Paul to the Corinthians:

Love is patient, love is kind. It is not jealous, [love] is not pompous, it is not inflated, it is not rude, it does not seek its own interests, it is not quick-tempered, it does not brood over injury, it does not rejoice over wrongdoing but rejoices with the truth. It bears all things, believes all things, hopes all things, endures all things.

Love never fails. If there are prophecies, they will be brought to nothing; if tongues, they will cease; if knowledge, it will be brought to nothing. For we know partially and we prophesy partially, but when the perfect comes, the partial will pass away. When I was a child, I used to talk as a child, think as a child, reason as a child; when I became a man, I put aside childish things. At present we see indistinctly, as in a mirror, but then face to face. At present I know partially; then I shall know fully, as I am fully known. So faith, hope, love remain, these three; but the greatest of these is love.

1 CORINTHIANS 13:4–13

The family's Bible may be used for an alternate reading such as John 15:9–12.

The reader concludes:

The Word of the Lord.

All respond:

Thanks be to God.

After a time of silence, all join in prayers of intercession for the couple and for others. All recite the Lord's Prayer. Then the engaged couple may exchange rings or some other gift that signifies their pledge to each other. One of the parents may bless these gifts:

N. and N., in due course may you honor the sacred pledge symbolized by these gifts which you now exchange.
R. Amen.

Parents may then place their hands on their child's head in blessing. One or more of the parents speaks the blessing:

We praise you, Lord,
for your gentle plan draws together
    your children, *N.* and *N.*,
in love for one another.
Strengthen their hearts,
so that they will keep faith with each other,
please you in all things,
and so come to the happiness of celebrating
    the sacrament of marriage.

We ask this through Christ our Lord.
R. Amen.

All make the sign of the cross as the leader concludes:

May the God of love and peace
abide in you, guide your steps,
and confirm your hearts in his love,
now and for ever.
R. Amen.

*The blessing may conclude with song. The following may be sung
to a tune such as "The Old Hundredth" ("Praise God from Whom
All Blessings Flow").*

From all that dwell below the skies,
Let the Creator's praise arise;
Let the Redeemer's name be sung,
Through ev'ry land by ev'ry tongue.

In ev'ry land begin the song;
To ev'ry land the strains belong;
In cheerful sounds all voices raise,
And fill the world with loudest praise.
                    ISAAC WATTS

BLESSING OF A SON OR DAUGHTER BEFORE MARRIAGE

Before the wedding, the family may gather around its member who is to be married, perhaps at a special meal in the family's home.

All make the sign of the cross. A parent begins:

Let us bless the Lord,
by whose goodness we live
and by whose grace we love one another.
Blessed be God for ever.

All respond:

Blessed be God for ever.

Then the scripture is read:

Listen to the words of the book of Deuteronomy:

Hear, O Israel! The LORD is our God, the LORD alone! Therefore, you shall love the LORD, your God, with all your heart, and with all your soul, and with all your strength. Take to heart these words which I enjoin on you today. Drill them into your children. Speak of them at home and abroad, whether you are busy or at rest.

DEUTERONOMY 6:4–7

The reader concludes:

This is the Word of the Lord.

All respond:

Thanks be to God.

The parents may give a Bible to the one who is to be married. Then all join in prayers of intercession for the couple to be married and for the world. After the Lord's Prayer, the parents and other family members place their hands on the head of their son/daughter as one parent speaks the blessing.

May the Lord, who gave you into our care
and made you a joy to our home,
bless you and keep you.
R. Amen.

May the Lord, who turns the hearts of parents to their children
and the hearts of children to their parents,
smile on you and be kind to you.
R. Amen.

May the Lord, who delights in our love for one another,
turn toward you and give you peace.
R. Amen.

All make the sign of the cross as the leader concludes:

May the God of love and peace
abide in you, guide your steps,
and confirm your heart in his love,
now and for ever.
R. Amen.